GRAPHIC BIOGRAPHIES

ELEANOR ROOSEVELT
FIRST LADY OF THE WORLD

by Ryan Jacobson

illustrated by Gordon Purcell
and Barbara Schulz

Consultant:

F. Kennon Moody, PhD

Roosevelt Family Researcher

Lagrangeville, New York

Capstone *press*

Mankato, Minnesota

Graphic Library is published by Capstone Press,
151 Good Counsel Drive, P.O. Box 669, Mankato, Minnesota 56002.
www.capstonepress.com

032011
006127R

Library of Congress Cataloging-in-Publication Data
Jacobson, Ryan.
    Eleanor Roosevelt: First Lady of the world / by Ryan Jacobson; illustrated by Barbara Schulz
and Gordon Purcell.
        p. cm.—(Graphic library. Graphic biographies)
    Summary: "Describes the life and work of U.S. First Lady Eleanor Roosevelt"—Provided
by publisher.
    Includes bibliographical references and index.
    ISBN-13: 978-0-7368-4969-2 (hardcover)   ISBN-10: 0-7368-4969-6 (hardcover)
    ISBN-13: 978-0-7368-6193-9 (softcover pbk.)   ISBN-10: 0-7368-6193-9 (softcover pbk.)
    1. Roosevelt, Eleanor, 1884–1962—Juvenile literature. 2. Presidents' spouses—United
States—Biography—Juvenile literature. I. Schulz, Barbara, (Artist) ill. II. Purcell, Gordon, ill. III.
Title. IV. Series.
E807.1.R48J34 2006

Art and Editorial Direction
Jason Knudson and Blake A. Hoena
Designers
Jason Knudson and Katherine Opseth
Illustrators
Gordon Purcell and Barbara Schulz
Editor
Angie Kaelberer

Editor's note: Direct quotations from primary sources are indicated by a yellow background.

973.917'09—dc22   2004028556
Direct quotations appear on the following pages:
Pages 7, 22, 23, 25, 26, from *The Autobiography of Eleanor Roosevelt,* by Eleanor Roosevelt
    (New York: Harper & Brothers, 1961).
Page 16, from *Eleanor Roosevelt: An American Conscience*, by Tamara K. Hareven
    (Chicago: Quadrangle Books, 1968).
Page 11, from Franklin and Eleanor Roosevelt Institute, http://www.feri.org.
Page 18, from Penn Library Exhibitions: Marian Anderson: A Life in Song,
    http://www.library.upenn.edu/exhibits/rbm/anderson/linimage.html.
Page 21, from *Eleanor and Franklin: The Story of Their Relationship, Based on Eleanor
    Roosevelt's Private Papers*, by Joseph P. Lash (New York: Norton, 1971).
Page 27 (top), from the Eleanor Roosevelt Memorials, Franklin D. Roosevelt Library,
    Hyde Park, New York.
Page 27 (bottom), from the National Park Service, http://www.nps.gov.

Cover illustration shows Eleanor's trip in 1933 to investigate working conditions in the coal mines
of West Virginia.

Table of Contents

Chapter 1
Little Nell

In 1892, 7-year-old Eleanor Roosevelt's life was filled with sadness. Her father, Elliott, had been in a hospital for a year. Her mother, Anna, was often sick with headaches.

Rest your head, Mama. I'll take care of you.

I miss Papa! I can't wait until we are together again.

Eleanor loved her mother and was happy to care for her. But Eleanor believed her father was the only person who loved her. He called her "Little Nell."

The next year brought more sadness. Eleanor's mother and her middle brother died. Eleanor moved into her grandmother's house with her youngest brother. Her only happiness came from her father's visits.

Will you visit again soon, Papa? I miss you so much.

Little Nell, soon I'll come back all well and strong. We'll have such good times together.

But the happy life Eleanor's father promised never happened. He died a year later. Eleanor was only 9.

Life will never be the same again.

In 1914, many European countries began fighting World War I. The United States entered the war in 1917. By then, Franklin was assistant secretary of the Navy. Eleanor helped organize the Navy Red Cross.

It seems like all we ever do these days is knit.

But we are doing such important work. Each stitch will help keep a soldier warm.

By 1918, the war was over. Franklin and Eleanor visited Europe early the next year.

Look at the terrible results of war. This was once a peaceful village!

So many people dead. So many buildings destroyed.

Franklin and Eleanor were right. In 1928, Franklin became governor of New York. In 1932, he was elected President of the United States.

At the time, the country was experiencing the Great Depression. Many Americans were poor and without jobs.

This great nation will endure as it has endured, will revive, and will prosper . . .

This depression is the worst thing that's ever happened to us. How can one man fix everything that's wrong with this country?

Listen to what President Roosevelt has to say.

. . . The only thing we have to fear is fear itself.

11

Later, Eleanor visited a cloth factory. She was shocked to see children working there.

Why aren't you in school?

I've never been to school. I work here to help my family.

When she returned to Washington, Eleanor told Franklin what she had learned.

Children work all day, until they are too tired even to stand! They should be in school. We must do something to help them.

I'll see what I can do.

In 1938, Franklin signed the Fair Labor Standards Act. This law said children younger than 16 years old could not work in factories.

Thousands of people wrote to Eleanor asking for help. She tried to help as many of them as she could.

This young woman has a crooked back and can't find work!

I'm going to send this letter to the Orthopedic Hospital in New York. Maybe they can help the poor girl.

Eleanor arranged for free medical treatment for the young woman, Bertha Brodsky. Bertha was just one of many Americans who received help from Eleanor.

I'm so glad to meet you, Bertha.

Thank you for helping me. Soon, I'll be well enough to get a job.

15

In 1939, a famous African American singer, Marian Anderson, was scheduled to perform at Constitution Hall in Washington, D.C. But the Daughters of the American Revolution (DAR) wouldn't allow Marian to sing at the hall. Eleanor was a member of the DAR.

This hall belongs to the DAR. We can't let a person of her race perform here.

How can you silence a great voice just because of the color of its owner's skin?

I'm resigning from the DAR!

But Eleanor didn't stop there. She helped set up a concert in front of the Lincoln Memorial. More than 75,000 people came to hear Marian Anderson sing.

. . . From every mountainside, let freedom ring!

Chapter 4
First Lady of the World

In October 1945, 50 countries formed an organization to work for world peace and human rights. It was called the United Nations.

President Truman just called. He asked me to be an American delegate for the United Nations!

But I have no background or experience in international meetings!

Mother, you can do it! It's what Father would have wanted.

You're right. I'll do it.

Eleanor was a kind, caring person. But she could get angry, especially when someone criticized the United States.

We are not here to attack each other's governments, and I hope when we return on Monday, the delegate of the Soviet Union will remember that! Meeting adjourned!

Eleanor presented the Universal Declaration of Human Rights to the United Nations General Assembly in 1948.

THE UNIVERSAL DECLARATION OF Human Rights

People from all nations, both men and women, now have the right to live free of discrimination, get an education, worship as they please, and have a fair trial.

Within months, the declaration was approved. Today, it is still thought to be one of the most important documents ever written.

25

Eleanor retired from the United Nations in 1953. As she grew older, she became weak from all of her work.

Mother, you really must slow down. The boys agree with me.

But there is so much to do; so many heartbreaking and pressing needs.

Eleanor remained concerned about young people and their problems. She helped raise money for a school for troubled boys. Each year, she hosted a picnic for the boys.

Mrs. Roosevelt, please read to us again!

Rikki-tikki-tavi was a mongoose, with fur and a tail like a cat's and a head like a weasel's . . .

More about ELEANOR ROOSEVELT

- Eleanor was born October 11, 1884, in New York City. Her full name was Anna Eleanor Roosevelt.

- Eleanor's uncle Theodore Roosevelt was the 26th President. He served from 1901 to 1909.

- In the late 1920s, Eleanor helped run the Todhunter School, a private high school for girls in New York City. Eleanor taught classes at the school and also served as its principal for a time.

- Before Eleanor became first lady, most presidents' wives were not a part of politics. But Eleanor changed that. She was the first to fly in a plane, to have a government job, to meet with Congress, to be paid for speaking in public, and to talk on the radio. Eleanor was also the first president's wife to write a daily newspaper column, *My Day*.

- To help women get better jobs, Eleanor sometimes held press conferences where only women were invited. Newspapers had to hire women reporters if they wanted to get the story.

When Eleanor joined the United Nations in 1946, she was the only female member. Most of the other members thought she should not have been there. But her hard work won over the other delegates.

 In February 1962, President John F. Kennedy named Eleanor to the President's Commission on the Status of Women. She served on the committee until her death from tuberculosis November 7, 1962.

 Val-Kill, Eleanor's home in Hyde Park, New York, is the only National Historic Site dedicated to a first lady. Visitors can see Eleanor's cottage, her gardens, and her yard.

GLOSSARY

committee (kuh-MIT-ee)—a group of people who meet to solve a problem or do certain tasks

delegate (DEL-uh-guht)—a person who is sent to represent a group or an organization

governor (GUHV-urn-or)—the leader of a state's executive branch of government

polio (POH-lee-oh)—a disease that attacks the nerves, spinal cord, and brain

tuberculosis (tuh-bur-kyuh-LOH-siss)—a serious and contagious lung disease caused by bacteria

INTERNET SITES

FactHound offers a safe, fun way to find Internet sites related to this book. All of the sites on FactHound have been researched by our staff.

Here's how:

1. Visit *www.facthound.com*
2. Type in this special code **0736849696** for age-appropriate sites. Or enter a search word related to this book for a more general search.
3. Click on the **Fetch It** button.

FactHound will fetch the best sites for you!